MARY
QUEEN of SCOTS

MA=   RIA.

Regina   Scotia.

'In my End is my Beginning'

*Embroidered by Mary Queen of Scots on the royal cloth of state
which hung over her head, above her chair,
during her years of captivity.*

ABOVE:

Mary was born 'a very weak child, and not likely to live as it is thought,' in the palace of Linlithgow, and baptized in the Church of St Michael. The birth was not welcome; 'All men lamented that the realm was left without an heir to succeed', as Knox put it.

RIGHT:

The palace of Linlithgow, once a 'palace of pleasance', is now in tranquil ruins.

For the first six years of the young queen's life those who contested the control of her person and destiny were more immediately interested in her Scottish kingdom than in her long-term chances of the English throne. The two chief rivals in the field were the rulers of France and England. Henry VIII was the first to act. Eager to subject Scotland permanently to his authority he proposed a marriage between his young son Edward, now aged five, and the new-born Scottish queen. When Edward eventually succeeded his father in England the two thrones would be united. Meanwhile, Mary would be brought to England and Henry would govern Scotland in her name. In this way centuries of Anglo-Scottish feuding would be brought to an end and the northern frontier of England made secure.

The natural alternative to an English marriage for Mary was a French one. The 'auld alliance' between France and Scotland was of long standing and rested on the very firm foundation of a shared desire to check the expansionist ambitions of the English kings. Francis, Duke of Guise, and Charles, Cardinal of Lorraine, young Mary's uncles, were soon to be the leading men in that country. They sought to raise the fortunes of their family still further by marrying their little Scottish niece into the French royal house. Henry II, who became King of France in 1547, readily fell in with the Guise family schemes and offered as bridegroom his own eldest son, the Dauphin Francis, two years Mary's junior. A dynastic union such as this would make permanent the political link with Scotland

and very effectively keep England in check.

From the Scottish point of view a union of the French and Scottish thrones would as effectively subject Scotland to an alien power as would a union with England, but in the 1540s subjection to the old ally France seemed preferable to subjection to the old enemy England. For this reason the French marriage was agreed to and the young Queen of Scotland was sent to France.

Thus ended the first turbulent chapter in Mary's life. When she sailed from Dumbarton on 7 August 1548 she was not yet six years old, and can have had very little notion of the political power struggles that had centred upon her almost since her birth.

The next ten years were comparatively uneventful. Mary grew to maturity in the sheltered environment of the French royal nursery, the daily playmate and constant companion of her young husband-designate. Much of her time was spent at the palace of Fontainebleau, or at the great royal chateaux on the Loire, Blois and Chambord. Her days passed pleasantly; schooling was interspersed with games and outdoor recreations. It was probably during these years that she acquired her lifelong passion for hunting.

During these same years her future seemed secure. When they were old enough she would marry Francis, for whom she early

LEFT:
Mary of Guise, second wife of James V of Scotland and mother of Mary. She sent her daughter to France for her education whilst governing Scotland in her name.

BELOW:
Mary wrote this letter at the age of 11 to her mother in Scotland. She normally wrote letters in French and signed herself MARIE.

developed a deep, but probably sisterly, affection. In due course, when his father died, he would be king and she would be queen of France. Scotland, that remote northern land of which she was already titular queen, was probably very seldom in her thoughts.

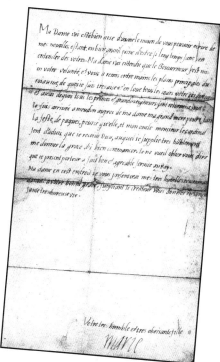

*I*n 1558 events began to move again. In April, when she was not yet sixteen and he was barely fourteen, Francis and Mary were married in the Cathedral of Notre Dame in Paris. In November, when Mary Tudor died in England, the French King, Henry II, arguing that her half-sister Elizabeth was illegitimate and could not inherit the English throne, advanced the claim of his recently acquired daughter-in-law, the young Queen of Scotland, to be also Queen of England in succession to her lately deceased cousin and namesake.

In July of the following year King Henry died from wounds inflicted accidentally in a 'friendly' bout of jousting and Mary of Scotland now reached the pinnacle of her regal career in three kingdoms; queen-regnant of Scotland; queen-consort of France; queen-claimant of England.

This early challenge by Mary to the position of Elizabeth I is important in helping to explain the English queen's later attitude to her Scottish cousin. There is a grisly irony in the fact that Mary's claim to be Queen of England in Elizabeth's place came originally from the French king who on first seeing her had declared, 'The little Queen of Scots is the most perfect child that I have ever seen.' Could he perhaps be said to be the original author of her destruction? Mary, a little over a year and a half later, was content enough to acknowledge Elizabeth's title and to seek no more than recognition as her heir, but Elizabeth could never forget this initial attempt to exclude her from her father's throne. While Mary lived there was always the chance that someone would press her claims again. Mary was a standing threat to Elizabeth's personal security.

Mary did not long enjoy her triple queenship. In July 1560, by the Treaty of Edinburgh, she was required to abandon her claim to be queen of England. In December of the same year her weakly husband died from an uncontrolled infection of the ear and was succeeded by his younger brother Charles. As a childless widow Mary was now of no account in France. All that was left to her was her original Scottish throne.

> *If there be not in her a proud mind, a crafty wit and an indurate heart against God and his truth, my judgement faileth me.*
>
> JOHN KNOX (TO HIS FRIENDS)

But Scotland itself had undergone a revolution. In 1559, in the name of the reformed religion, and aided by the fiery preaching of John Knox and by arms and money from England, a group of Scottish nobles, the self-styled Lords of the Congregation, had overthrown the government of the Regent, Mary's mother. They had then summoned the Scottish Parliament and remodelled the Scottish Church on Protestant lines. What sort of reception would these new masters of the Scottish kingdom give to the eighteen-year-old queen in whose name they still professed to govern, she who had been brought up in the French court, firm in the traditional Catholic faith? It says a great deal for Mary's courage that she was prepared to put this question to the test. On 14 August 1561 she sailed from Calais and returned to Scotland, after an absence of thirteen years.

ABOVE:
Chambord, one of the Loire chateaux at which Mary spent such a happy childhood.

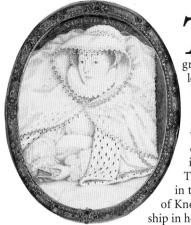

ABOVE:

Mary Queen of Scots as a Widow *by Nicholas Hilliard (1547–1619). White was the French colour for mourning and it suited Mary's colouring admirably.*

The Scots received their new queen at first with caution and then with growing pleasure. Her good looks and stately bearing (she was notably tall for a woman of her generation) won their hearts, her tragic young widowhood aroused their compassion, her moderation overcame their fears. Though she quietly insisted, in the face of the fulminations of Knox, upon her right to worship in her own way, she was plainly no crusading Catholic bigot come to sweep away the recent reformation. And she soon had allies among the ruling lords.

One of the leaders of the Lords of the Congregation was Mary's illegitimate half-brother, the Lord James Stewart, better known by his later title of Earl of Moray. In the initial stages of the negotiations for the Queen's return to Scotland he had a prominent part to play. He visited her in France and impressed upon her the need to accept the recent religious changes in her kingdom. At the same time he spoke out strongly for her own right, if she so wished, to continue to hear masses in the privacy of her royal chapel, and established with Mary a mutual confi-

dence which was to be the foundation upon which her early successes in Scotland were to rest. For Mary *was* at first a great success. The invective of Knox, who was quite incapable of extending to her religious views the degree of tolerance she accorded his, and the shadows of later disasters tend too often to obscure the fact that for the first few years after her return to Scotland in 1561 Mary played the very difficult role of Catholic queen in a recently protestantised country with tact, with charm and with energy. She also, though she was still little more than a girl, managed to keep a very effective check upon the ambitions and rivalries of her quarrelsome and turbulent nobles. In this latter task the support of Lord James, twelve years her senior, was invaluable.

And yet, however successful she may have been in tackling the many problems that beset her as queen, there was one that she most lamentably failed to solve, and that was the question of her marriage. She would, of course, have to take a husband. No woman could rule alone. (Elizabeth I had not yet been long enough on the throne of England

RIGHT:

James Stewart, Earl of Moray and Mary's half-brother, became her trusted adviser.

RIGHT:

A page of Knox's 'Blast' against female rulers published at Geneva in 1558, three years before Mary returned to 'beare rule' in Scotland.

THE FIRST BLAST 9
TO AWAKE WOMEN
degenerate.

O promote a woman to beare rule, superióritie, dominion or empire aboue any realme, nation, or citie, is repugnāt to nature, cótumelie to God, a thing moſt contrarious to his reueled will and approued ordināce, and finallie it is the ſubuerſion of good order, of all equitie and iuſtice.

In the probation of this propoſition, I will not be ſo curious, as to gather what foeuer may amplifie, ſet furth, or decore the fame, but I am purpoſed, euen as I haue ſpoken my conſcience in moſt plaine ād fewe wordes, ſo to ſtād content with a ſimple proofe of euerie membre, bringing in for my witneſſe Goddes ordinance in nature, his plaine will reueled in his worde, and the mindes of ſuch as be moſte auncient amongeſt godlie writers.

And firſt, where that I affirme the em-

to prove the exception to that current generalisation.) Every queen needed the strength and support of a husband to uphold her authority in what was a man's job in a man's world. It was, of course, also the duty of every queen to provide for the future security of her kingdom by producing an heir. The question therefore was not 'Should Mary marry?' but 'Whom should she marry?'

Nor was this a question that affected Mary and Scotland alone. England and Elizabeth were also deeply concerned about it. While Elizabeth remained unmarried Mary had a very strong claim to be acknowledged as her heir, and so the man Mary married might one day be not only King of Scotland but King of England, or at least the father of an English king. Elizabeth never openly accepted Mary as her heir for there were other claimants to be considered and, as a matter of policy, the English queen preferred to keep the question open. But it was clear from the close interest that she took in the problem of finding a husband for Mary that Elizabeth did regard this as a matter of major moment for her subjects and herself.

RIGHT:

Henry Stuart, Lord Darnley, probably painted shortly before his murder.

RIGHT:

The Queen's beauty was admirably set off by white lace before the trials of her life took away her youthful bloom.

For Mary's hand there was no shortage of suitors. As queen of one country with a good claim to be heir to another she was the best available bargain in the international marriage market. Spanish and Imperial princes were strongly fancied, but Elizabeth disapproved. Alien princes meant alien influences, and alien influences (other than English) in Scotland were to be discouraged. As an alternative candidate Elizabeth, somewhat surprisingly, and at first a little coyly, suggested her own first favourite, Robert Dudley, now raised to the peerage as Earl of Leicester to make him more acceptable. But Mary would have none of him.

In the end Mary herself chose to marry Henry, Lord Darnley, eldest son and heir of the Earl of Lennox, and her own first cousin. It would appear, on Mary's part, to have been a genuine love match. So captivated was she by his outward charm that she totally failed to see behind it to the shallow self-indulgent and ambitious character that his attractive exterior concealed.

> ### *I know not, but it is greatly to be feared that he can have no long life among these people.*
>
> THOMAS RANDOLPH,
> ENGLISH AMBASSADOR, OF DARNLEY.

The Darnley marriage was Mary's great mistake and the beginning of her tragic downfall. Outwardly the young man, who was nearer to her in age than any of the other candidates for her hand, had everything to recommend him. He came of royal lineage on both sides. His mother, born Margaret Douglas, was a daughter of Mary's grandmother, Margaret Tudor, by a second marriage. His father was descended from a junior branch of the royal house of Stewart. His claim to the English throne was almost as good as Mary's and was immeasurably strengthened by his marriage to her. Their son was James VI who was eventually to follow Elizabeth on the English throne.

But Darnley was young and spoiled by an ambitious mother. He lacked the strength of character and was incapable of the selfless devotion to his wife's interests which was so necessary to help her through the difficult situation resulting from the jealousies which her marriage so naturally produced. Indeed, his pride and insensitivity only served to

LEFT:
The royal palace of Holyroodhouse, drawn in 1647 by J. Gordon of Rothiemay.

BELOW LEFT:
Mary Queen of Scots stayed frequently at Craigmillar Castle, three miles south-east of Edinburgh. Its remains date from the 14th to the 17th centuries.

BELOW:
David Rizzio, Mary's Italian secretary, was one of the 'sly crafty foreigners' hated by the Scottish nobles for their intimacy with the Queen. He was considered small, ugly and 'ill-favoured' but his loyalty was beyond reproach and this earned him her affection.

aggravate a situation which would have been difficult enough without them. And in the end his gullibility made him the easy victim of ruthless men's intrigues.

The most immediate and serious consequence of Mary's marriage to Darnley at Holyrood on 29 July 1565 was that it broke the working partnership between herself and Moray. He who had supported her so faithfully since her return to Scotland and who had become, because of the high esteem in which the queen held him, virtually the first man in the kingdom, now found himself pushed aside in favour of the new young king, a callow, selfish youth, who was, moreover, the son of Moray's ancient rival, Lennox. Moray rebelled, was outlawed and fled to England.

It was not easy for Mary to find a substitute for Moray. It soon became very clear to her that Darnley was not the man to counsel or advise. Interested only in the power and opportunities his newly-acquired royalty gave him, he had no thought for the responsibilities which his position involved. Nor could any other Scottish noble measure up to the stature of Moray. Mary had a natural horror of disloyalty, as shown by Moray on whom she had heaped honours and goods, but her Italian secretary, David Rizzio, appointed in 1564, was a man whom she could trust absolutely. Mary's private passion was music and Rizzio was a talented musician and an amusing conversationalist. It was not long before he earned the jealousy of Mary's husband by playing cards late into the night with her.

The love affair with Darnley did not last. Mary's pregnancy contributed to its ending. The physical discomfort she endured was not compensated for by any increase in husbandly concern. When she could no longer ride or hunt he continued to pursue such pleasures on his own. The blindfold of infatuation was lifted from her eyes. She saw him now for what he was, a self-indulgent playboy, given over too frequently to drink. Mary ceased even to delight in his company on the rare occasions when he offered it. Estrangement grew between them as rapidly as the original affair.

Darnley, for his part, grew suspicious. His wife no longer doted on him. She no longer lavished gifts upon him or pandered to his whims. She kept the exercise of the regal power increasingly to herself, though earlier she had been eager to associate him as king with her in all her acts. It was easy in these circumstances for jealous nobles, plotting mischief, to focus Darnley's attention upon Rizzio who seemed now to be well established in the confidence of the queen, and to persuade him to give his full support to the plot they were hatching to assassinate the Italian secretary.

On the night of 9 March 1566, while Mary sat at supper in Holyroodhouse, Darnley unexpectedly entered the queen's apartments by means of the private stairway from his own suite on the floor below. Hardly had the queen's party, which included Rizzio, recovered from this unexpected intrusion when the other conspirators followed by the same route, seized the secretary, dragged him struggling and protesting from the room and savagely stabbed him to death outside.

The motives of the participants in this violent deed were varied. For Darnley it was a comparatively straightforward act of vengeance against the man who, he believed, had supplanted him in the queen's affections. For others of the murderers the victim was a low-born upstart who had risen too high in the kingdom and was ousting better men from the positions of influence to which their birth entitled them. Some perhaps even entertained the hope that the shock of their barbarous deed would cause Mary, who was six months pregnant, to miscarry and even to die, leaving the way clear for Darnley to claim the kingdom in his own right. Thereafter, they could hope to share in the spoils and to rule the kingdom through their influence over him. Mary herself chose to believe afterwards that her own life had been directly aimed at. For this she never forgave Darnley, though she chose to take no action before the birth of her child.

The murder of Rizzio solved nothing. The gulf between Mary and Darnley grew even wider as she learned more fully of the extent of his complicity in the crime. The disaffected nobles who had hoped to profit with Darnley from the elimination of the Italian were soon as anxious to be rid of him and his pretensions. He was an embarrassment to all parties including the queen. His private life became if anything more scandalous and dissolute. Something would have to be done about him. But Mary concealed the depth of her revulsion from her husband until the child was born. For the future security of her throne and kingdom it was vital that neither the life nor the legitimacy of that child should be put at risk.

LEFT:
Falkland Palace was inhabited briefly by Mary Queen of Scots and her baby son, James.

BELOW:
The double portrait of Mary and her son James VI was painted in 1583 from imagination by an unknown artist, since Mary last saw James as a ten-month-old infant.

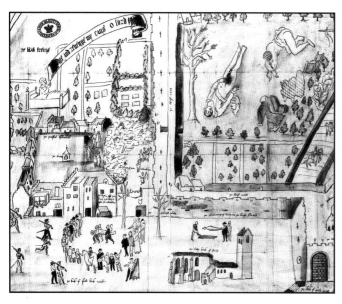

ABOVE:

A contemporary sketch of the murder of Darnley at Kirk o' Field, showing the bodies of Darnley and his servant (top right), Darnley's body being borne to the provost's lodging (bottom left) and his baby son James in his cradle (top left).

RIGHT:

The only known portrait of James Hepburn, Earl of Bothwell. A violent, ambitious nobleman, he aimed at replacing Darnley as the Queen's consort. Later, witnesses accused him of having personally set light to the gunpowder under Darnley's rooms. A few months after the murder, he abducted Mary and married her.

P rince James, Mary's only child and Darnley's son, was born on 19 June 1566. When Mary had recovered somewhat from the birth and from the nearly fatal illness that afflicted her a few months later, she was readier to act. With a party of nobles (which included Moray, now restored to favour, and Bothwell, whose staunch support at the time of Rizzio's murder had been invaluable to her) Mary, in late November, discussed the problem of her husband. The possibility of divorce was raised and dark hints were dropped of 'other means'. There is, however, no certain evidence that Mary was at any time a party to the plans that now began to be laid against the life of Darnley, but neither is there any positive evidence that she was not. The whole affair of Darnley's death is one of the most intractable mysteries of history, and every account of it leaves some loose ends. Even the way he died is not quite clear. The house, at Kirk o' Field in Edinburgh, in which he was staying on the night of 9–10 February 1567, was totally destroyed by an explosion at 2 a.m., but Darnley's body was found in a garden on the other side of the town wall, strangled!

What matters to Mary's story is not how Darnley died, or who killed him, but what her contemporaries believed at the time. Popular report ascribed the leadership in the con-

spiracy against Darnley to James Hepburn, Earl of Bothwell. When, therefore, a bare three months after the murder, on 15 May 1567 Mary married this same Bothwell, Scotland was scandalised.

On the face of it, this marriage to a man thought to have been responsible for the murder of an unwanted and inconvenient husband does seem scandalous. But Mary saw Bothwell as a loyal and strong supporter at a time when she was so wracked by melancholy and despair that she could make no important political decisions sensibly. All her other advisers had deserted her, intent on saving their own skins in the coming political débâcle. Bothwell persuaded several of the most powerful Scottish nobles to sign a document saying that if the Queen would accept him as a husband the signatories would promise to promote the marriage by counsel, vote or assistance. After a short interval Bothwell began to pay suit to Mary, on the basis that he was the man the nobles thought most suitable to be king. Queen Mary always asserted afterwards that she refused him because of the scandals about Darnley's death.

A little later Mary, returning to Edinburgh from Stirling Castle where she had been visiting her baby, was met by Bothwell and about 800 men. He said danger was threatening in Edinburgh and he would take her to the castle of Dunbar for safety. She meekly agreed, rather than be the cause of bloodshed. Once there Bothwell implemented the last part of his plan: 'The Queen could not but marry him, seeing he had ravished her and laid with her against her will.' It must be remembered that at this time Mary's health was poor and her state of mind fatally indecisive; she prob-

ably felt that Bothwell's strength of personality was exactly what she needed to help her govern Scotland. And so, on 15 May, just over 3 months after the death of Darnley, Mary married Bothwell at Holyrood, according to a Protestant rite and with none of the preparations she so loved.

The public reputation of the queen was tarnished beyond recovery by her third marriage. Many of her people were quite ready now to believe that she had actually and delib-

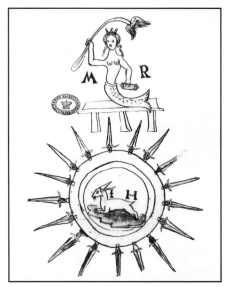

LEFT:
This insulting propaganda placard appeared in Edinburgh soon after Darnley's murder. It shows Mary as a mermaid (the contemporary synonym for a prostitute), above a hare (Bothwell's family crest) surrounded by daggers.

erately participated in the plot against Darnley in order to clear the way for Bothwell. Some were beginning to wonder if there would ever be peace in Scotland with this shameless woman on the throne who seemed by her very presence there to invite conspiracy, intrigue and murder. Others began to think that the infant James might offer a better alternative. If he could be set up as king and a regency established to rule in his name, there might be some hope of achieving stability.

This was the plan eventually adopted by the group of Scottish nobles who 'rescued' Mary from Bothwell at Carberry Hill on 15 June 1567, and then very promptly shut her up a prisoner in lonely Lochleven Castle. There they forced her to sign a deed of abdication and to name a council of regency for her infant son.

On 29 July 1567 James VI was crowned King at Stirling and, in August, Mary's half-brother Moray was proclaimed Regent. Moray thus appears to be the ultimate beneficiary of all the conspiracies and murders of the preceding two years. He had discreetly avoided direct involvement in both the Rizzio and the Darnley affairs, and even more discreetly retired to England during the rise and fall of Bothwell. Now he returned to assume a position of power even greater than that he had enjoyed as Mary's confidant before Darnley had come on the scene. From 1567 to 1570, when he, in turn, fell to an assassin's bullet, he brought to Scotland an unaccustomed continuity in government.

Bothwell escaped capture in Scotland, but was forced to flee to Norway where he died insane in 1578, in prison.

ABOVE:
Lochleven Castle, Mary's prison for almost a year, had previously been the site of her honeymoon with Darnley.

ABOVE LEFT:
Borthwick Castle, in which Bothwell and Mary took refuge during the revolt against them. They left separately under cover of darkness, the Queen disguised as a boy.

ABOVE:
Dundrennan Abbey. Mary held her last council at Dundrennan on 16 May 1568 before seeking refuge across the Solway in England.

FAR RIGHT:
The exquisite silver casket in Lennoxlove Museum is believed to have contained the 'Casket Letters' – love letters said to have been written by Mary to Bothwell.

RIGHT:
A miniature of Mary Queen of Scots by Nicholas Hilliard made during the years 1575–80, probably for Mary's supporters during her captivity.

Mary's imprisonment in Lochleven lasted less than a year. On 2 May 1568, with the aid of sympathisers within the castle, she escaped and made a desperate bid to regain her throne. Defeated by the forces of the regent at Langside on 13 May she fled first to Dumfries and then across the Solway Firth to England, landing at Workington on 16 May.

Mary never set foot in Scotland again. For several years her restoration was not too remote a possibility, but one that would depend very much upon the attitude adopted by the English queen who now found herself faced with the problem of dealing with an uninvited and embarrassing royal guest.

Elizabeth's attitude to Mary was the product of conflicting impulses. The one object she had clearly in mind at all times was the need to keep Scotland free from any undesirable alien influences. England's security was Elizabeth's first concern. Mary, who was so ready to appeal to the Pope, to the King of France or to the King of Spain for help in recovering her throne and who might still be persuaded to press her claim to England, was, from Elizabeth's point of view, a less desirable occupant of the Scottish throne than young James and his protecting lords who relied so heavily on English support to maintain themselves and their authority. But, on the other hand, Mary was rightful Queen of Scotland and Elizabeth could hardly approve of her deposition by her own subjects. That sort of precedent was not to be encouraged.

At one point, in October 1568, it looked as if Elizabeth was seeking a way out when she permitted representatives of the Scottish lords to participate in an enquiry into Darnley's death which was held by English commissioners, acting in their own queen's name, at York. If Mary was shown to have been a consenting party to the murder, perhaps then Elizabeth would accept the justice of her deposition. It was at this investigation that the famous silver casket, allegedly containing incriminating letters from Mary to Bothwell, was first produced. Elizabeth was not very much impressed by these, but did realise thereafter that the Scottish lords were determined to convict Mary and that if she were permitted to return to Scotland it would be almost certainly to trial, condemnation and execution. If, on the other hand, Elizabeth set Mary free and allowed her to go to France or Spain to seek support, she would be actively encouraging foreign intervention in Scotland of the kind she was anxious above all to avoid.

> *I am myself a Queen, the daughter of a King, a stranger, and the true Kinswoman of the Queen of England. I came to England on my cousin's promise of assistance against my enemies and rebel subjects and was at once imprisoned . . .*
> *As an absolute Queen, I cannot submit to orders, nor can I submit to the laws of the land without injury to myself, the King my son and all other sovereign princes . . . For myself I do not recognize the laws of England nor do I know or understand them as I have often asserted. I am alone, without counsel, or anyone to speak on my behalf. My papers and notes have been taken from me, so that I am destitute of all aid, taken at a disadvantage.*
>
> REPLY OF MARY TO COMMISSIONERS FOR TRIAL
> AT FOTHERINGHAY, 11 OCTOBER 1586.

Queen Elizabeth's dilemma over her Scottish cousin was so difficult that Mary remained for 18 years in forced residence in England. Her residences were many; Carlisle, Bolton, Chatsworth, Sheffield, South Wingfield, Coventry, Tutbury, Chartley and, finally, Fotheringhay.

Throughout the long years of her imprisonment Mary never gave up hope of securing her release. Repeatedly she asked for a personal interview with Elizabeth, confident that such a confrontation would swiftly resolve all difficulties and win Elizabeth's unqualified support. But Elizabeth steadily ignored her pleas and the two queens never met. In her very natural eagerness to be free Mary was willing to accept the aid of almost anyone prepared to offer it, and this lack of caution in her dealings with would-be rescuers was to be her ruin in the end.

The whole period of her imprisonment was punctuated by plots on her behalf. Some of the conspirators, such as the group of local Derbyshire and Lancashire gentry who planned to spirit her away from Chatsworth in 1570, were moved more by romance or hope of immediate reward than by any deepseated religious or political motivation. But other plots, especially those hatched after the papal bull excommunicating and deposing Elizabeth in May 1570, had more dangerous international ramifications.

When Pope Pius V decided at long last to move against Elizabeth, since there seemed no hope remaining that she would seek an accommodation with Rome, the rightful queen of England, both in foreign and in native Catholic eyes, was now the captive Mary. From then on most of the plots involving her had the same purpose and only the details varied. They all envisaged the elimination of Elizabeth, the release of Mary and

ABOVE:
The layout of Mary's trial at Fotheringhay Castle, 15 October 1586. Mary sat on a chair in the right of the room. The court consisted of earls (sitting on the left bench) and barons and knights of the Privy Council (right and centre benches).

For myself, I am resolute to die for my religion . . .
With God's help, I shall die in the Catholic faith
and to maintain it constantly . . .
My heart does not fail me . . .
Adieu, mon bon cousin.

QUEEN MARY, AT CHARTLEY, ON 21 SEPTEMBER 1585
ON BEGINNING OF JOURNEY TO FOTHERINGHAY.

NEAR RIGHT:
Elizabeth Talbot, Countess of Shrewsbury, better known as 'Bess of Hardwick', was the domineering wife of Mary's keeper, George, Earl of Shrewsbury.

FAR RIGHT:
The Earl of Shrewsbury kept Mary in custody on his estates in Derbyshire at Sheffield, Chatsworth and Wingfield from 1569–84. He allowed her to take exercise and distribute alms to the local poor, and even to take the waters at Buxton.

RIGHT:
In January 1585 Mary was removed to Tutbury where she was strictly confined, her attendants reduced in number, her correspondence censored and access to her person rigorously controlled.

RIGHT:
Mary loved to embroider and during her long years of captivity made many pieces of work such as these panels now in the Palace of Holyroodhouse, Edinburgh.

her elevation to the English throne. The more dangerous of the plots also involved the invasion of England by a foreign force, usually Spanish. None of these conspiracies was in itself really serious. Most of them were uncovered in good time, but their effect was cumulative. The more often the Queen of Scots was shown to be the focus for subversion, the more eagerly Elizabeth's loyal subjects pressed for her elimination. The more frequent the plots the more difficult it was for Elizabeth to resist the pressure on her to act. The circumstances of the Babington conspiracy of 1586, in which Mary tacitly conceded to the assassination of Elizabeth, made it impossible.

Queen Elizabeth sought to avoid responsibility for the death of her cousin, Mary Queen of Scots, but she herself was a victim of the political opinions and pressures of the day.

In 1585 Parliament had passed an act making mandatory the trial of any person on whose behalf a plot against the Queen's life might be devised. Mary had to be tried, and the evidence of her complicity brought forward at her trial could not be ignored. Her conviction followed swiftly, and only the Queen's clemency could then save her from the sentence of death that the court imposed.

Yet still Elizabeth had hesitated to take any irreversible action. Only under pressure from her councillors did she permit a warrant for Mary's execution to be prepared. Only under pressure did she sign it. And only, according to her own account, against her will and without her knowledge was that warrant finally dispatched and acted on.

On the evening of Tuesday 7th February 1587 Mary Queen of Scots was informed that

Well, Jane Kennedy, did I not tell you this would happen? . . .
I knew they would never allow me to live, I was too great an obstacle to their religion.

QUEEN MARY, ON HER LAST NIGHT.

she would die the following morning at eight o'clock. After a frugal supper Mary methodically went through all her possessions – money, clothes, jewels and personal mementos such as silver boxes, miniatures and enamelled tablets, and divided them up for her servants and for royal relatives abroad.

She then drew up an elaborate will by which she hoped to provide for the welfare of her servants and the poor children and friars of Reims. Her own spiritual welfare was considered in a farewell letter to her chaplain, of whose presence she was deprived in her last hours. In it she made a general confession of all her sins. Finally, she wrote to her brother-in-law, King Henry of France,

ABOVE:
Mary Queen of Scots with her attendants, Jane Kennedy and Elizabeth Curle, receiving the news of her death sentence. Her reply was dignified: 'I thank you for such welcome news. You will do me great good in withdrawing me from this world out of which I am very glad to go.'

relating the circumstances of her death. All this preparation took until two o'clock in the morning. At six she arose from her bed, on which she had merely rested but not slept, and went into her oratory to pray.

At eight she was sent for. Mary was quite calm and some observers described her afterwards as cheerful and smiling. In the entry chamber to the hall her servants were held back; on Elizabeth's orders she was to die alone. Melville, her steward, fell on his knees in tears, but Mary gently reprimanded him: 'You ought to rejoice and not to weep for that the end of Mary Stuart's troubles is now done.

Thou knowest, Melville, that all this world is but vanity and full of troubles and sorrows. Carry this message from me and tell my friends that I died a true woman to my religion, and like a true Scottish woman and a true French woman …' In the event, Mary having given her word that her servants would not cry out or try to seize relics of blood-stained cloth, six of them were allowed to be present at her death.

The axe rose and fell, and Mary was no more. There is no doubt that in the end it was under the Queen of England's authority that the Queen of Scotland died.

'Rue not my death, rejoice at my repose
It was no death to me but to my woes:
The bud was opened to let out the rose,
The chain was loosed to let the captive go.'

FROM *DECEASE, RELEASE*, ODE BY ROBERT SOUTHWELL,
ON THE DEATH OF MARY QUEEN OF SCOTS.

MARIA SCOTIÆ REGINA GALLÆ DOTARIA REGNORUM ANGLIÆ ET HYBERNIÆ VERÆ PRINCEPS LEGITIMA IACOBI MAGNÆ BRITANIÆ REGIS MATER, A SVIS OPPRESSA ANNO DNI 1568 AVXILII SPE ET OPINIONE A COGNATA ELIZABETHA IN ANGLIA REGNANTE EMISSI EO DESCENDIT, IBIQVE CONTRA IVS GENTIVM ET PROMISSI FIDEM CAPTIVA RETENTA, POSTCAPTI VITATIS ANNO 19, RELIGIONIS ERGO, EIVSDEM ELIZ. PERFIDIA ET SENATVS ANGLICI CRVDELITATE, HORRENDA CAPITIS LATA SENTENTIA NECI TRADITVR, AC 12 CAL. MARTII 1587 IN, AVDITO EXEMPLO A SERVILI ET ABIEC TO CARNIFICE TETRV N MOREM CA PITE TRVNCATA EST. ANNO ÆTATIS REGNIQVE 45

IOANNA ELIZABETHA KENNETHIE. CVRLE.

...ANIA FODRINGHAMII.

REGINAM SERENISSᵐ REGVM FILIAM, VXOREM ET MATREM, ASTANTIBVS COMMISSARIIS ET MINISTRIS R. ELIZABETHÆ, CARIFEX SECVRI PERCVTIT ATQ, VNO ET ALTERO ICTV TRVCVLENTER SAVCIATÆ TERTIO EI CAPVT ABSCINDIT,

PRIMA QVOAD VIXIT COL. SCOT. PARENS ET FVND.

SIC FVNESTVM ASCENDIT TABVLATVM REGINA QVONDAM
GALLIARV ET SCOTIÆ FLORENTISᵐᵃ INVICTO SED PIO
ANIMO TYRANNIDEM EXPROBRAT ET PERFIDIAM.
FIDEM CATOLICAM PROFITETVR ROMANÆ ECCLESIÆ

LEFT:
The memorial portrait commissioned by Mary's lady-in-waiting, Elizabeth Curle: on the left is the execution scene and on the right Jane Kennedy and Elizabeth Curle.

RIGHT:

All the places shown on the map have a connection with Mary Queen of Scots. She herself never travelled further south than Fotheringhay Castle, but her final resting place is in Westminster Abbey.

BELOW:

Mary's youth was happily spent in the great chateaux of the Loire.

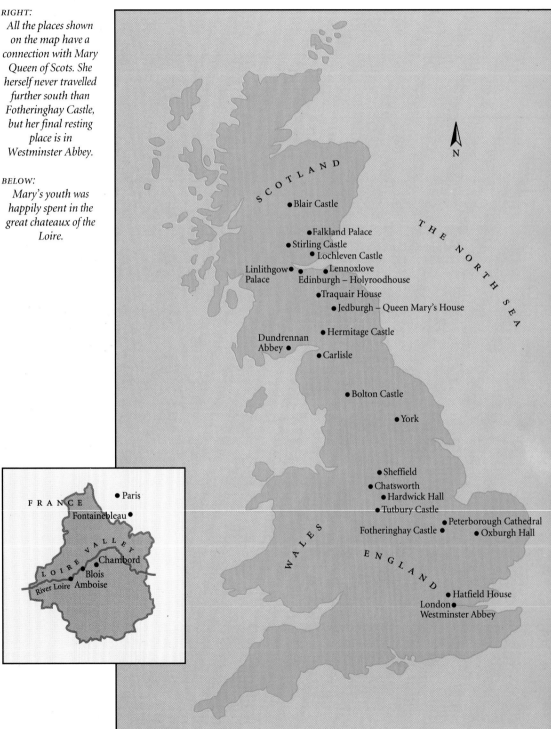

SCOTLAND

● Blair Castle

● Falkland Palace
● Stirling Castle
● Lochleven Castle

Linlithgow ● ● Lennoxlove
Palace Edinburgh – Holyroodhouse

● Traquair House
● Jedburgh – Queen Mary's House

THE NORTH SEA

Dundrennan ● Hermitage Castle
Abbey ●
● Carlisle

● Bolton Castle

● York

● Sheffield
● Chatsworth
● Hardwick Hall
● Tutbury Castle

● Peterborough Cathedral
Fotheringhay Castle ● ● Oxburgh Hall

WALES

ENGLAND

● Hatfield House
London ●
Westminster Abbey

N

FRANCE
● Paris
Fontainebleau ●

LOIRE VALLEY
● Chambord
Blois ●
River Loire Amboise